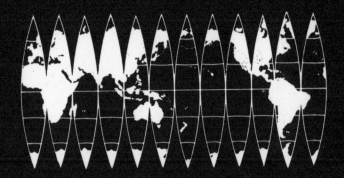

Editor in Chief • PHILLIP BACON

Professor of Geography
Teachers College, Columbia University

Managing Editor • JOANNA ALDENDORFF   Picture Researcher • PETER J. GALLAGHER

Associate Editor • PETER R. LIMBURG   Cartographer • VINCENT KOTSCHAR

Picture Editor • ROBERT J. GARLOCK   Designer • FRANCES GIANNONI

Staff • JUDY KORMAN, BARBARA VINSON, KATHLEEN SEAGRAVES, JOHANNA GREENWALD

Special Section of Statistical Maps • RICHARD EDES HARRISON

Covers • RAY PIOCH

Complete List of Books

These books tell the exciting story of how people live in all parts
of the world. You will see how men use the land for farming and
industry. You will learn about mountains and deserts, oceans
and rivers, cities and towns—and you will discover how the
daily life of people in other countries compares with your own.

BOOK 5

AFRICA

BY NORMAN LOBSENZ

THE GOLDEN BOOK

PICTURE ATLAS

OF THE WORLD

IN SIX VOLUMES

Illustrated with More than 1,000 Color Photographs and Maps

GOLDEN PRESS · NEW YORK

Millions of Africans live in villages like this one in Northern Rhodesia. The round huts have grass roofs.

THIS IS AFRICA

The continent of Africa rises out of the waters of the Atlantic and the Indian Oceans. From its northern tip in the sunny Mediterranean Sea to the storm-lashed Cape of Good Hope at the south, Africa stretches for 5,000 miles.

All told, the continent covers 12,000,000 square miles. This makes it the second biggest of the world's seven continents. (The largest is Asia.) Africa's area is one fifth of all the land on earth—as much as the United States, Western Europe, China, and India put together.

This huge land mass is shaped roughly like a giant question mark. And this is very appropriate. For, apart from the coastal regions, most of the country was unknown until about 100 years ago. Many men had tried to learn Africa's secrets. But the geography of the continent made it difficult.

For one thing, Africa's coastline is smooth and unbroken by the curving bays and sharp peninsulas that other continents have. Ships found it difficult to get through the rough surf and close to the shore.

Even Africa's rivers do not provide waterways into the heart of the continent, for they drop to the oceans from a high central plateau by means of waterfalls and rapids. These obstacles bar the way to boats coming upstream.

By land, too, the way was blocked. In some places deserts sprawl their burning sands and rocks for thousands of miles. In others, dense jungle makes travel almost impossible. And even those parts of the coast where a man can land are usually rocky or swampy.

Yet some brave explorers dared all these dangers. They crossed the blazing deserts and penetrated the deadly swamps and jungles. And they brought back stories of strange people and animals, mighty rivers and lakes, great plains, and awesome mountains.

Today we are really just beginning to discover Africa—to learn about its beauty, its tremendous natural resources, and the many different ways in which its 225,000,-000 people live.

AFRICA

Scale 1:30,000,000

0 100 200 300 400 500 Miles

⋇ **ALEXANDRIA** *Cities over* 1,000,000 *population*
⊙ Algiers *Cities of 250,000 — 1,000,000 population*
○ Luanda *Cities under* 250,000 *population*
● *Capitals of Countries*

Depths in feet: Heights in feet:
over 650   0-650   Below sea level   0-650   650-1650   1650-4900   over 4900

Intermittent streams
Head of navigation
⋈⋈⋈ *Wadi*   *Salt Lake*   *Desert*
——— *Railroads*   —·— *Canals*   *Swamp, marsh*

An Arab shepherd boy tends his flocks on an Algerian hillside that slopes to the Mediterranean Sea.

Africa is a land of great geographical variety. The central region of the continent is covered by the great rainforest. Footpaths and rivers are the only "roads" that can cut through the thick growth of plants and trees. Taller trees interlace their branches to form a green canopy over the smaller trees below.

On either side of the rainforest are the savannas. They are broad, flat, 600-mile-wide plains that lie between the rainforest and the desert areas to the north and south. The region of the savanna nearest to the forest has tall grass, shrubs, and trees. But as the savanna land approaches the desert it becomes treeless. Only short grass and stunted bushes break the broad sweep of the plain. Most of Africa's game animals live in the savanna lands—antelope, zebra, giraffe, elephant, lion, rhinoceros.

North of the equator the savanna is called the Sudan. It stretches from the Atlantic coast in the west to the Red Sea in the east. The Sudan has given its name to two countries: the Sudanese Republic in West Africa and the Sudan in East Africa, south of Egypt.

The grasslands south of the equator are called the *veld*, a Dutch word meaning "field." The veld is bounded on the south and west by a very dry region known as the Kalahari Desert.

But the Kalahari is just a "baby" desert compared to the enormous Sahara, which borders the northern savanna.

The Sahara is the biggest desert in the world. It extends from the Atlantic Ocean, on Africa's west coast, to the Red Sea on the east coast—a distance of 3,000 miles. From north to south it is 1,000 miles wide. Roughly, the Sahara accounts for nearly one third of the entire continent.

Beyond the two deserts are the coastal strips. Northern Africa, cut off from the rest of the continent by the Sahara, is a lofty plateau of farmland cut diagonally by mountain ranges. The land slopes gradually toward the shores of the Mediterranean Sea. At the Strait of Gibraltar, where Africa reaches out toward Europe, the continents are only eight miles apart. South of the Kalahari Desert a similar coastal strip, also fringed by farmlands and mountains, forms Africa's southern tip.

Slightly more than two fifths of the continent is covered by grassland, and slightly less than one fifth by forest. The other two fifths is desert. Within these broad areas of forest, savanna, desert, and coast there are many striking features. In East Africa, the land rises into highlands with dead volcanoes towering above them. Even though they are almost directly on the equator, Mt. Kilimanjaro (19,565 ft.) and Mt. Kenya (17,040 ft.), are topped the year around by a mantle of snow. And nearby is the East African Rift, a deep north-south valley in the earth which stretches for thousands of miles. Parts of it are filled by lakes and craters.

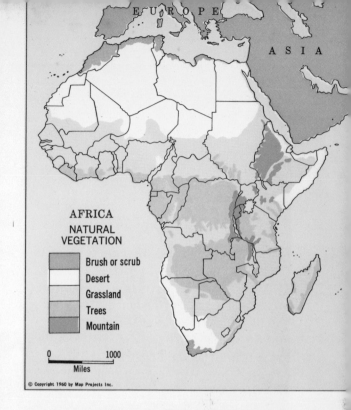

AFRICA
NATURAL
VEGETATION

- Brush or scrub
- Desert
- Grassland
- Trees
- Mountain

0   1000
Miles

© Copyright 1960 by Map Projects Inc.

Ethiopia, a land of rugged highlands and mountains, is surrounded by hot, dry lowlands. Because of its height, Ethiopia receives considerable rainfall, enough to support lush forests and meadows.

W. Kuls

Africa is considered unique among the continents in that it consists of a single great chunk of rock. Some experts think the basic rock of Africa was formed 200,000,000 years ago. Geologists, who study the structure of rocks, have noticed that Africa's rock is very much like the kind of rock found in eastern Brazil, the peninsula of India, and the western part of Australia.

Men studying maps have always been fascinated by the idea that these parts of the earth, now widely separated by great oceans, may once have been part of the same land mass. For instance, the bulging "shoulder" of Brazil would seem to fit neatly into the Gulf of Guinea, where West Africa extends into the sea. Similarly, the western coasts of India and Australia "fit" into parts of Africa's east coast.

Some geologists believe that more than 200,000,000 years ago all these lands were part of a single ancient continent, which they have named Gondwanaland. Millions of years ago, they think, great upheavals of the earth broke Gondwanaland into several separate land masses, the beginnings of the continents we know today.

Mighty rivers pour through the heart of Africa. Five of them drain almost two thirds of the continent. For many hundreds of miles, the rivers move sluggishly through marshlands or rainforests, fed by thousands of tributary streams. Then, as the waters begin their downward journey from the central plateaus, the rivers pick up speed. Some hurl themselves over immense waterfalls. Others make the descent in a series of short, steep drops, or rapids, which make navigation impossible.

Only a few stunted shrubs manage to live in this vast sand-dune region of the sprawling Sahara Desert.
Conzett and Huber

The two Niles—the Blue and the White—flow into each other at Khartoum to form Africa's greatest river. Egypt's flourishing agriculture depends on the water of the Nile for irrigation.

The longest of Africa's rivers—and the longest in the world if it is measured from its first source—is the Nile. From its headwaters at Lake Victoria to its mouth in the Mediterranean Sea, the Nile is about 4,100 miles long.

The Nile is actually two rivers. The White Nile is born in the jungle rainwaters which drain into Lake Victoria, near Tanganyika. As it flows northwest it is joined at Khartoum, in the Sudan, by the Blue Nile. The Blue Nile rises in Lake Tana, high in the mountains of Ethiopia. The Nile curves through the Nubian Desert, drops sharply in a swift series of six rapids, and then flows through Egypt. At this part of its journey the Nile is as much as 10 miles wide. Beyond Cairo the river begins to separate into many mouths, which form its delta leading into the Mediterranean.

Africa's second longest river is the Congo. Its 2,718 miles drain a great basin of one and a half million square miles in central Africa. In some places the Congo is so wide that it splits into many arms. In its journey from the central plateau, the Congo drops over several rapids and two waterfalls. The Congo is the only African river that crosses the equator twice. There are more than 4,000 islands in the river.

The Niger River is 2,600 miles long. It is the third longest in Africa. For many years explorers sought to trace the course of this mysterious river. They thought it moved westward to the Atlantic Ocean. Actually, it rises in the mountains only 200 miles from the Atlantic and flows toward the east. But then it swings in a wide loop northward into the Sahara Desert. The Niger's floodwaters make it possible to grow rice and cotton in the region around Timbuktu. Then the Niger turns southward through Nigeria. It finally reaches the sea in the Gulf of Guinea. Its delta spreads across 200 miles of marshy coast. The first

Bushes, trees, and vines fight for sunlight in the overgrown depths of the forest in Uganda.

Conzett and Huber

Kilimanjaro, Africa's highest mountain, rears its snow-covered summit nearly four miles into the sky.

white man to see the Niger was a Scottish explorer named Mungo Park, who reached it near the native city of Ségou.

The 1,600-mile Zambezi River forms the border between Northern and Southern Rhodesia. It flows through the heart of the Federation of Rhodesia and Nyasaland to the Indian Ocean. Like the Congo, it drains a huge basin in the central plateau. Near the town of Livingstone, the Zambezi plunges over Victoria Falls at the rate of 47,000,000 gallons of water per minute. Because of the continual booming of its water and the clouds of spray that it creates, the local tribes call Victoria Falls "the smoke that thunders."

Southern Africa's chief river is the Orange. It flows 1,300 miles from east to west, crossing the Union of South Africa to empty into the Atlantic Ocean. The river flows through part of the Kalahari Desert. But in this area its bed may be dry except during flood seasons. As a result, the river is useless for either navigation or irrigation. There are several important diamond deposits near its mouth.

A rainbow arcs across clouds of spray from the thundering waters of Victoria Falls, where the Zambezi River plunges 347 feet into a narrow, rocky gorge. The falls are Africa's outstanding tourist attraction.

P. Popper Ltd.

Martin S. Klein

Mountain craters reveal the volcanic origin of the Canary Islands, off Africa's northwest coast.

There are some fascinating islands off the coasts of Africa.

Madagascar is a huge island off the southeastern Africa coast, in the Indian Ocean. Now known officially as the Malagasy Republic, it is a part of the French Community. It is nearly 1,000 miles long and as much as 360 miles wide. It is the fourth largest island on earth, ranking after Greenland, New Guinea, and Borneo.

Zanzibar is a 640-square-mile island just off the coast of Tanganyika. It is a British protectorate and is ruled by a sultan. Zanzibar produces most of the world's supply of cloves.

South of the western bulge of Africa are some small islands. They are the tops of dead volcanoes that rise above the ocean, Fernando Po is the island capital of Spanish Guinea. Cocoa and coffee are its chief crops. Two Portuguese islands, São Tomé and Principé, have fine plantations. But they also serve as prison camps, where convicts are sent to work out their sentences.

Of the west coast are the Cape Verde Islands. Volcanic and extremely dry, they are a stopping point for boats going between Africa and South America. The Canary Islands are also a transatlantic crossroads. Their pleasant climate draws many visitors. Farther out in the Atlantic and considerably to the north are the Madeira Islands. The main island is beautiful, with terraced hillside gardens which yield delicious fruits, colorful flowers, and the grapes that make the famous Madeira wine, once very popular in England.

The waters of the Atlantic and the Indian oceans join at Africa's southern tip, the Cape of Good Hope, once called the Cape of Storms. Today many South African coastal areas are popular beach resorts.

Martin S. Klein

Courtesy of the South African Tourist Corporation

A herd of zebras drink at a South African waterhole. They keep a wary lookout for prowling lions.

ANIMALS OF AFRICA

Africa is the only place in the world where so many different kinds of wild animals still exist. Some of these animals are well known — lions, elephants, gorillas, zebra, camels, giraffes. We can see them all alive in the zoo, or as part of a museum display. But there are many other creatures in Africa which are seldom seen anywhere else. The aardvark, for example, has long ears, a thick tail, sharp claws, and a long snout. It is about as big as a pig. With its

claws the aardvark (a word meaning "earth pig") opens the tall mounds which are termite nests, and scoops up thousands of termites with its long, sticky tongue. Some animals inhabit specific regions. The Congo is the home of the gorilla. The lemur, a tiny monkey, swings in the forests of Madagascar. The gray parrot—the kind that can be taught to talk—lives mostly in West Africa. The jackass penguin (its cry sounds like a donkey's bray) waddles

The evil-tempered camel snarls and groans at its master. But it carries huge loads across the desert.

Raymond Bricon

Giant anthills like the one shown below provide food for the termite-eating aardvark.

Kerwin B. Roche—House of Photography

Gatti—FPG

Courtesy of the South African Tourist Corporation

"Rhinoceros" is Greek for "horn-nosed." When a rhino twitches his ears, he is about to charge.

Russ Kinne—Photo Researchers

African waters teem with crocodiles. They can lie motionless for hours or move with lightning speed.

Here are some interesting facts about a few African animals:

A full-grown hippopotamus may be 14 feet long and five feet high at the shoulder. The hippo may weigh up to four tons and can stay under water as long as ten minutes. Hippos often travel overland by night to eat the crops of native farmers.

Lions live and hunt in family groups called "prides." Males are lazy, and the female must do all the hunting and killing.

The ostrich averages 8 feet in height, weighs 300 pounds, and can run 20 miles an hour.

The five most dangerous animals are the lion, the leopard, the rhinoceros, the elephant, and the buffalo. The fiercest of these is a wounded buffalo.

The cheetah is considered to be one of the fastest four-footed animals. It has been clocked over short distances at speeds of more than 60 miles an hour.

An elephant herd plunges into a stream to bathe. The huge beasts eat 1,000 pounds of food a day.

Alfred G. Milotte

Raymond Bricon

A stern Tuareg—a dweller in the desert—rides his camel. His turban also serves as tie and scarf.

THE PEOPLE OF AFRICA

Scientists divide the peoples of Africa into five chief groups:

1. Arabs, who live mostly in Egypt and North Africa.

2. The Hamites, who occupy Ethiopia and much of the Sahara.

3. The "true" Negroes who live in West Africa and the Sudan.

4. Isolated primitives: the Bushmen of the Kalahari Desert, the Hottentots of southwest Africa, and the Pygmies of the Congo.

5. The Bantus, Negro people who occupy much of central and southern Africa.

In addition, there are about 5,000,000 whites of European stock in Africa. Most of them live either along the North African coast, or in South Africa.

In the long history of Africa many of these peoples and races have intermarried, creating even further mixtures.

Many Africans still worship tribal gods. But nearly 90,000,000 are Moslems, who pray to Allah. About 30,000,000 have become Christians as a result of the work of missionaries.

This Libyan boy cradles his pet, a baby gazelle, in his arms. The tiny antelope lives in the desert.

Charles Erikson—Shostal

About 225,000,000 people live in Africa. They are of many different colors and races. There are hundreds of different tribal groups. And these people speak at least sixteen separate major languages, each with many different-sounding dialects.

This tremendous variety makes for energy and progress. But it also is a handicap to understanding and cooperation.

Paul Hufner—Shostal

Raymond Bricon

Berbers, the chief native race of North Africa, are noted for their skill as horsemen. These men are armed with old-fashioned brass-bound muskets.

Top: a water vendor fills a drinking cup. Water vendors are the chief source of drinking water in this dry land.

Bottom: an Arab shepherd, muffled against the wind, tends his flock in the mountains.

Wolfe Worldwide Films, Los Angeles 24, Calif.

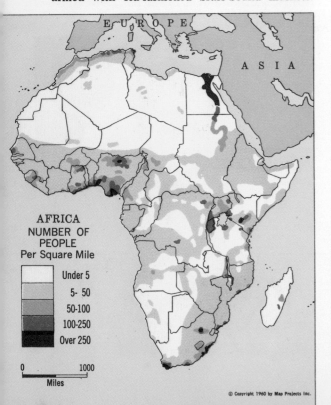

AFRICA
NUMBER OF
PEOPLE
Per Square Mile

	Under 5
	5- 50
	50-100
	100-250
	Over 250

0   1000
Miles

© Copyright 1960 by Map Projects Inc.

Paul F. Milhollan

An Egyptian child in native costume stands on a Cairo sidewalk.

Barefooted boys pass in front of the Coptic cathedral in Addis Ababa, Ethiopia's capital.

Elizabeth Morton—American Museum of Natural History

For a long time men used to think that the "Garden of Eden" was somewhere in central Asia. But today some scientists who specialize in the history of mankind tend to believe that the first human beings developed in Africa.

Bones of apelike creatures with some human characteristics have been found in remote parts of Africa. Perhaps they are the long-sought "missing links" in the evolution of man.

Even though the rest of the world knew very little about most of Africa until only 200 years ago, important races and cultures flourished there thousands of years ago. (Culture means the way of life of a group of people.) One theory holds that the fertile regions of northeast Africa were the original birthplace of these early civilizations.

Sometime around 3,000 B.C. the Sahara dried out into the desert that it is today. It formed an almost impassable barrier between the Mediterranean coast area of Africa and the interior of the continent. But some peoples did manage to cross it, either in search of new lands or under the pressure of conquerors from Europe and Asia.

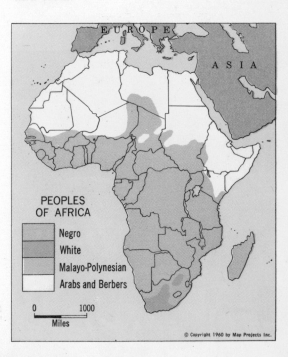

PEOPLES OF AFRICA

Negro
White
Malayo-Polynesian
Arabs and Berbers

0   1000
Miles

© Copyright 1960 by Map Projects Inc.

Erich Kolmar—Shostal

Above: villagers in the Sudan build their round huts in a circle about a central clearing.

Below right: a typical house of northern Ghana

Below left: the opening of Ghana's Parliament

Stephanie Dinkins—FLO

Stephanie Dinkins—House of Photography

Sheridan H. Garth

Watusi tribesmen are the world's tallest people. Warriors like these may reach a height of 7 feet.

The people who moved southward from the Sahara and the Nile started civilizations of their own. They became the ancestors of the many tribes of Africa today. Because of the different environments they lived in, wide variations in their cultures developed. Some tribes became metalworkers. Others farmed the land or became herders. Some lived by hunting. Although almost every tribe had artists who made statues and magical masks, the designs of the carvings varied from tribe to tribe.

Conflicts often arose between tribes that followed different ways of life. Hunters, herders, and farmers all competed for the best land. Often the settled farmers were raided by nomadic hunters or herders. Constant warfare was the rule over large sections of Africa.

Charles Trieschmann—Camera Clix

A boatman strains at his huge oar to steer his dugout across the Uélé River in the Belgian Congo.

FPG

Two Pygmy youngsters practice their drumming.

Tom Larson—American Museum of Natural History

A woman of a Bushman tribe tends her children.

Wolfe Worldwide Films, Los Angeles, 24, Calif.

In her best clothes, an Ndebele girl grinds corn.

Tom Larson—American Museum of Natural History

A Hottentot child stands before his hut.

Two Zulu women proudly display their beadwork.

Courtesy of the South African Tourist Corporation

A Wachagga woman carries bananas to market.

Elvajean Hall

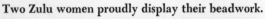

Dan Weiner—Rapho

Many Indians live in South Africa. These youngsters eat their lunch in a slum street in Durban, Natal.

The white residents of Johannesburg represent Africa's largest concentration of people of European descent.

H. E. Street—Shostal

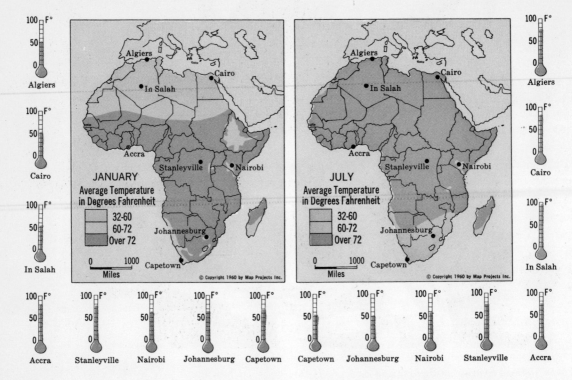

These maps show the average temperature and rainfall of Africa. The symbols around the edge are keyed to important African cities. You will see that the temperature of a place does not necessarily correspond to its distance from the equator. You will also notice that south of the equator the seasons are reversed. Midsummer there is in January, and midwinter comes in July.

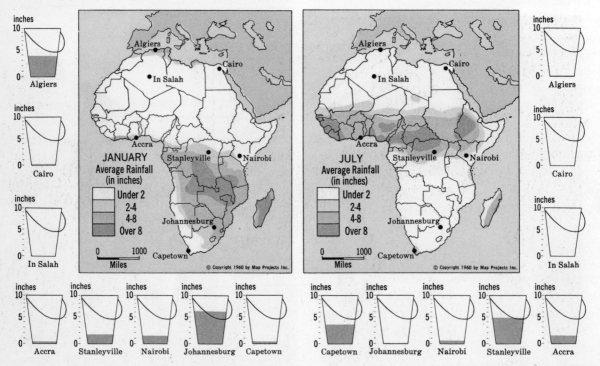

CLIMATE AND LAND USE

Africa's climate is strongly influenced by the continent's position on the globe. Three fourths of Africa's territory (about 9,000,000 square miles) lies within the tropics. The climate of this huge region ranges from warm to hot—except where high altitude lessens the heat. The only real seasons are the wet and dry seasons.

Let us look at the main climatic zones, shown on the map page at the left. They more or less correspond to the great plant-life belts, for plant life depends on moisture and warmth. Along the equator the rainfall is heavy and the weather is always warm. Temperatures range from 70 to 90 degrees and there is rain even in the "dry" season. As the land rises toward the east, both temperature and rainfall become less. In July, the average temperature in mile-high Nairobi is twenty degrees lower than the temperature at Freetown, which is at a similar latitude, but in the west coastal lowlands. The highest mountains, like Kilimanjaro, are snow-capped all year round.

Rainfall gradually decreases on each side of the equator. In the savannas there are definite dry and wet seasons. Cool weather alternates with warm. Because of the high temperatures, the savannas dry up in the dry season. Some trees lose their leaves. The ground becomes too dry for raising crops.

Contrary to what you may think, the hottest temperatures in Africa are not found at the equator, but in the deserts to the north and south. The highest temperature officially recorded in the world, 136 degrees, was recorded in the Sahara. It is reported that the surface of the ground may exceed 170 degrees. These temperatures are hot enough to cause the rocks of the desert to crack. But the Sahara is a place of great contrasts. The temperature may drop as much as sixty degrees at night. Frost is quite common in the winter months in the northern regions. As you might expect from the lack of vegetation, the desert climate is extremely dry. In places, rainfall is almost nonexistent. In some areas it does not rain for years at a time. When the rain does fall, it is liable to come in swift and violent storms, which cause local floods. Conditions in the southern desert are like those in the Sahara, but much less severe.

The northern and southern coastal strips of Africa have a "mediterranean" type of climate, with hot, dry summers and cool, rainy winters. Because of the rainfall distribution, most crops are raised in the winter. Summer crops depend on irrigation.

Peasants in loose gowns unload a cargo of sugar cane and grain from a Nile sailing vessel.

Joe Barnell—Shostal

W. R. Donagho—Shostal

Workers with machetes cut sisal leaves and pile them on flat-cars for transport to a coastal port.

Until new food plants were introduced by the Europeans, the African Negro peoples grew only millet (a kind of coarse cereal) and some rice. Peanuts, manioc, potatoes, corn, yams, coconuts, cacao, and bananas were brought from America. Citrus fruits came from Portugal. Wheat and barley also came from Europe. Tobacco came from America. The date palm was brought by the Arabs, who also brought the clove trees to Zanzibar in the nineteenth century.

Fronds of the date palm are a familiar North African sight. The tree usually signals an oasis.

Paul Hufner—Shostal

Some of the most important plants raised in Africa are:

SISAL—this plant of the agave family grows mainly in East Africa. Its hard fiber is used for twine and rope.

OIL PALM—the soft, reddish wax yielded by the fruit of this West African tree is used to make soap, candles, and grease. It is also important in the local diet.

DATE PALM—this is the familiar tree of the desert oases. It can grow to a height of 100 feet. When a date palm is 30 years old, it will bear 200 pounds of dates a year.

KOLA TREE—the juice of the brown nuts of this tropical African tree is used in making "cola" drinks.

CACAO—about 80 years ago an African returning from the island of Fernando Po brought with him half a dozen cacao beans and planted them on his farm in West Africa. Today this region produces about two thirds of the world's cacao. The seeds of this small tree are fermented, dried, roasted, and ground before being made into chocolate and cocoa. The fat or "butter" ex-

A Liberian slices into the tough bark of a rubber tree, preparing to tap the valuable liquid latex.

Courtesy of the Firestone Tire and Rubber Company

tracted from the seeds is used for fine soap and cosmetics. The country of Ghana is the largest single producer of cacao. Every other chocolate in every box of candy in the world comes from Ghana.

GUM ARABIC—this colorless gum comes from the acacia plant of East Africa's grasslands. It is used in glues and other adhesives, inks, candies, and medicines.

SORGHUM—this is one of the many cereal grasses of Africa. Because it can grow in dry areas, it is an important food crop. Some kinds of sorghum that grow in South Africa have a sweet juice, used for syrup. A bristly variety of sorghum is used to make whiskbrooms.

RUBBER—wild rubber was once a principal export of Africa, but now most African rubber is grown on plantations. The main source of rubber is the country of Liberia, where American companies own huge estates. Some rubber is also raised on plantations in the Belgian Congo.

As you can see from the map and the text on the preceding pages, the use of the land in Africa is determined mostly by climate and environment.

In the northern areas bordering the Mediterranean, the fertile valleys make good farm land. Cereals such as wheat and barley, and fruits like figs, grapes, and olives grow well.

Nearer to the Sahara, farms give way to the tent camps of nomads, who drive their sheep from place to place in search of water and grazing land. Only in the oases does anything grow. Here Arab or Berber families raise their date palms.

The broad areas of the savanna can grow millet and corn, tobacco, and cotton. Rice is raised near rivers. In the drier areas of savanna land, some tribes breed sheep, horses, and cattle.

Large-scale spraying with DDT today is exterminating the tsetse fly, and reclaiming millions of acres of land for farming or for grazing.

Bernheim-Conant, AMNH—FLO

Tribesmen from regions south of the Sahara come to the cotton market at Ft. Lamy, Chad Republic.

East Africa produces coffee. Its healthy highlands have many plantations. Cattle grazing is also important.

The oil palm, the peanut, and the cacao tree are the main crops of West Africa.

The continent also has tremendous stores of mineral wealth, most of it still unexploited. South Africa is famous for its diamonds and its gold. Not so well known are the immense copper mines of the Belgian Congo. Other important minerals are tin ore, iron ore, chromium, manganese, cobalt, uranium, and bauxite, the basic source of aluminum.

A native farmer in Sierra Leone prepares to harvest the last of the year's cacao crop.

British Information Service

EXPLORING THE AFRICAN CONTINENT

Our knowledge of Africa comes from the discoveries of many explorers—daring adventurers, naval and military men, peaceful traders, and dedicated missionaries. A few of the most important African explorers were these men:

GIL EANNES (Portuguese) sailed past Cape Bojador on Africa's northwest coast (1434), opening the way to further exploration. Previously, European sailors had believed that the sea beyond Cape Bojador was filled with monsters and that the strong currents there would in any case prevent ships from sailing further.

NUNO TRISTÃO (Portuguese) discovered the mouth of the Senegal River (1445) and brought back news of green and fertile country beyond the desert.

DIOGO CÃO (Portuguese) discovered the mouth of the Congo River and claimed the region for Portugal (1482).

BARTHOLOMEU DIAS (Portuguese) rounded the Cape of Good Hope (1488).

VASCO DA GAMA (Portuguese) sailed around the Cape of Good Hope and up the east coast of Africa, reaching India (1498).

JAMES BRUCE (Scotch) traveled through Ethiopia and traced the course of the Blue Nile (1770-72).

MUNGO PARK (Scotch) traveled up the Gambia River and across the savanna lands to reach the Niger (1795-96). On his second trip (1805), he explored over 1,000 miles of the Niger before his death in the rapids at Bussa during a native attack.

HUGH CLAPPERTON (English) crossed the desert from Tripoli to Lake Chad and explored the central Sudan (1821). In 1825-27 he traveled north through the jungle from the Guinea coast, reaching the Niger at Bussa. He died at Sokoto.

RICHARD LANDER (English) followed the Niger from Bussa to its outlet (1830-31), proving it did not flow into the Nile or the Congo, as many geographers believed.

RENÉ CAILLIÉ (French) crossed the Sahara to Timbuktu disguised as an Arab (1827-28).

HEINRICH BARTH (German) explored and mapped the Sudan and parts of the Sahara (1850-55). The sole survivor of a British expedition, he carried on alone for months.

KRAPF and REBMANN (German missionaries) discovered Mts. Kenya and Kilimanjaro in eastern Africa (1848-49).

DAVID LIVINGSTONE (Scotch missionary) spent most of his life in Africa. Between 1849 and his death in 1873 he explored the Kalahari Desert, the Zambezi River, Lake Nyasa, the Shiré River, and the upper course of the Congo. He also discovered Victoria Falls in 1855.

HENRY M. STANLEY (English-American) made a famous trip to rescue Livingstone (1871). In 1874-77 Stanley followed the Congo down to its outlet, opening up the region for development.

PIERRE SAVORGNAN DE BRAZZA (French) explored the lower Congo region (1875-80).

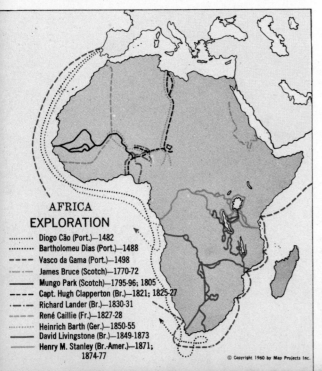

AFRICA
EXPLORATION

.... Diogo Cão (Port.)—1482
.... Bartholomeu Dias (Port.)—1488
– – – Vasco da Gama (Port.)—1498
– · – · James Bruce (Scotch)—1770-72
———— Mungo Park (Scotch)—1795-96; 1805
– – – – Capt. Hugh Clapperton (Br.)—1821; 1825-27
– · – · Richard Lander (Br.)—1830-31
– · · – René Caillié (Fr.)—1827-28
.... Heinrich Barth (Ger.)—1850-55
———— David Livingstone (Br.)—1849-1873
———— Henry M. Stanley (Br.-Amer.)—1871; 1874-77

© Copyright 1960 by Map Projects Inc.

CITIES
OLD AND NEW

The cities of Africa span thousands of years of history. The first cities were those of ancient Egypt — Alexandria, Thebes, Memphis. Then seafarers from Phoenicia, Greece, and Rome crossed the Mediterranean to found outposts on the North African shore such as Carthage and Tingis (now called Tangier).

Even hundreds of years after the Arabs conquered North Africa the only cities were those on the coast, and a few almost legendary towns that served as trading posts in the western Sudan. Timbuktu and Kano, in Nigeria, whose 1,000-year-old walls still stand, are two of the best known.

But today Africa can boast of dozens of major cities. Some are not as large or as thickly populated as those of Europe and America, but all are just as busy and just as modern.

These cities present a striking contrast between the old and the new Africa. Each

The mud-walled city of Kano, in northern Nigeria, has been an important trade center for 1,000 years.

Dakar, capital of the Senegalese Republic, has many modern sections. It is a major African port.

The world's largest mosque is in Cairo. This city has long been a center of Islam.

one has its "downtown" section. Modern office buildings, luxurious hotels, smart shops, and apartment houses line the broad streets. There are fine restaurants and cafes.

But only a mile or two away many Africans live as they have lived for hundreds of years. In the cities of North Africa, the "casbah," or native quarter, is still a crowded place of narrow, winding streets and heavily shuttered houses. Merchants still sell their goods from open stalls in the marketplace or "bazaar."

Not all of the new Africa is modern office buildings and luxurious hotels. There is much poverty and misery. Natives coming from tribal reserves often find it difficult to adjust to life in industrialized cities, and many of them must live in slums located in the hearts of big cities.

Hilly streets of Addis Ababa, Ethiopia's capital, descend from a waterway on the city's outskirts.

Raymond Bricon

Much of North Africa's trade is carried on in open-air market places like this one in Marrakesh, Morocco.

The modern city of Salisbury, capital and largest city of Southern Rhodesia, is located in the savanna.

Hans von Meiss—Photo Researchers

Courtesy of the South African Tourist Corporation

The city of Cape Town, South Africa, is spread out at the foot of dramatic, flat-topped Table Mountain.

Herbert Lanks—Monkmeyer

Bicycles, babies, and bundles highlight a street scene in Léopoldville, capital of the Belgian Congo.

Cotton waits for export on the docks of 2,300-year-old Alexandria, the chief port of Egypt.

Charles Trieschmann—Camera Clix

Veiled women walk the narrow streets of Tangier, an International Zone only 8 miles from Gibraltar.

Charles Trieschmann—Camera Clix

Courtesy of TWA—Trans World Airlines

Arched gateways and medieval battlements guard the ancient entrances to Tunis' Moslem quarter.

Johannesburg, Africa's third largest city, is surrounded by huge mounds of debris from its gold mines.

Martin S. Klein

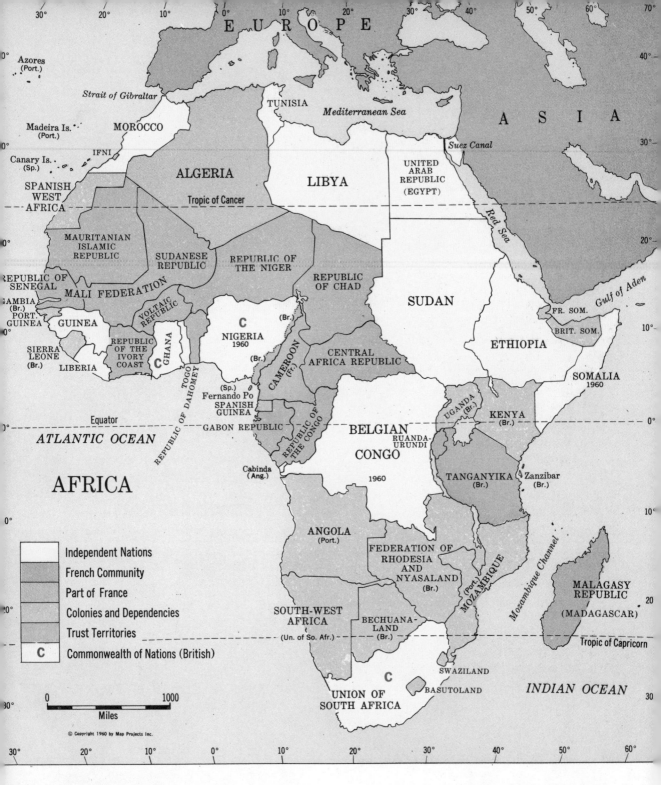

AFRICA

Legend:
- Independent Nations
- French Community
- Part of France
- Colonies and Dependencies
- Trust Territories
- **C** Commonwealth of Nations (British)

NOTE: Trust territories are areas administered by European nations under United Nations Supervision. South-West Africa, originally entrusted to the Union of South Africa, is now governed as a part of that country. Countries marked with a red C are British Commonwealths (former British colonies that have become independent). They are linked to Britain and each other by mutual treaties and common loyalty to the British Crown. The French Community states are former French colonies, now self-governing in internal affairs. They may leave the Community and become completely independent at any time, and also form unions between themselves within the Community, such as the Mali Federation. The President of France is also President of the French Community.

Transportation

Transportation in Africa is a vivid contrast between ancient and modern methods. Hunters on safari in the East African plains still use native porters. The men, strung out in a line, carry everything needed for the expedition in bundles on their heads. But at the same time, modern airplanes fly scheduled routes over Africa.

Fast, economical transportation is difficult in Africa for three reasons. One is the great distances involved. Another is the problem of building roads or railroads across deserts or through thick forests. A third is the shortage of skilled workers and materials.

Most of the main rail lines are in South Africa, North Africa, and Egypt. But perhaps the most important ones are the smaller railroads that link together the navigable stretches of Africa's rivers. The rivers are great highways for goods and people, but, as we have seen, most of the major rivers are broken by waterfalls or rapids. Boats cannot pass in either direction. So railroads have been built to carry passengers and freight around these "blockades."

Sturdy river steamers ply the Nile, the Niger, the Congo, and the other waterways. There are a few cabins, but most of the passengers usually live on the open decks.

Although many hundreds of miles of roads are being built in Africa, most of them are far from being modern highways. Very few of them are paved. In wet weather some of the roads are impassable. The roads still chiefly serve as "feeders," to enable people or goods to reach a river port or a rail head. Private automobiles are rare. Most traffic on the roads consists of buses or trucks.

Air travel is very important in present-day Africa. The airplane has cut travel time greatly and made possible the opening-up of many out-of-the-way areas. But the airplane has its limitations. It is very expensive to operate an airplane; so only

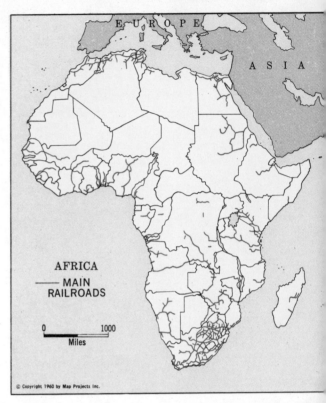

AFRICA
MAIN RAILROADS

0   1000
Miles

© Copyright 1960 by Map Projects Inc.

freight of great value in relation to its bulk can be carried. Most Africans cannot afford the passenger fare. Ordinary freight must go by rail, road, or water.

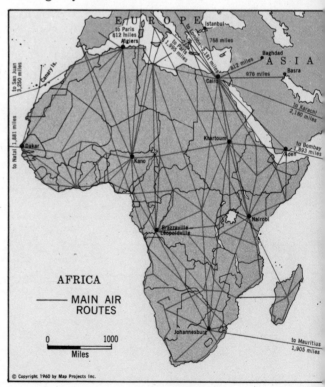

AFRICA
MAIN AIR ROUTES

0   1000
Miles

© Copyright 1960 by Map Projects Inc.

Morocco is an independent country slightly bigger than the state of California. Nearly 10,000,000 people live there, almost all of them Moslems. Morocco is ruled by a sultan. Its main commercial city is Casablanca. Rabat is the capital. Two of its most colorful ancient cities are Marrakesh and Fez.

Morocco's old walled cities and native quarters teem with veiled women and men in flowing robes and cloaks. The shops and market places are full of strange foods, rich silks, jewels, swords, and beautiful leatherwork. Sometimes magicians, jugglers, sword-swallowers, or fire-eaters perform in the bazaars. Camels, mules, and donkeys are led through the streets by their masters. And five times a day the muezzin—the priests of Allah—call the people to prayer from the tops of the mosques (Moslem houses of worship).

The fertile fields of Morocco yield harvests of wheat, barley, beans, and peas. The vineyards grow grapes that make good wine. Other crops include figs, almonds, citrus fruits, and olives.

A kind of wheat called semolina is used in a dish called *couscous*, the basic item in a Moroccan meal. In a heaping dish of the cereal there may be bits of everything from peeled grapes to meat and vegetables.

Where the land is drier, the people raise sheep and goats, cattle, horses, and camels. There is good fishing off the coast and Morocco has a large sardine-canning industry based on coastal fisheries.

The country is poor in metallic minerals. But it does have important deposits of natural phosphate rock, from which fertilizer is made.

Southwest of Morocco is Spanish West Africa, a desolate and almost useless patch of land on the shoulder of the continent. It is divided into two zones—Saguia el Hamra and Rio de Oro. The latter is a Spanish phrase meaning "River of Gold," but there is no gold nor river there. Offshore fishing provides the only income.

Charles May—Photo Researchers

An open square in Fez, Morocco, holds scores of huge wooden vats where leather goods are dyed.

Moslems in Rabat, Morocco, kneel and face the holy city of Mecca as they are called to prayer.

Paul Hufner—Shostal

A flock of sheep grazes contentedly in a Moroccan field. They find shelter from the blazing sun under the gnarled branches of a grove of olive trees. Olive oil is an important export of Morocco.

The Sidi Kacem refinery in Morocco refines oil from the important new fields in the Sahara.

A Moroccan girl with a baby on her back harvests wheat with a sickle, the method of Biblical times.

Ruins of Carthage's Roman amphitheater tell the story of ancient ties between Europe and Africa.

Tunisia lies on the northeast corner of Algeria. It is an independent republic about the size of New York State. Tunisia has about 3,800,000 people, nearly all of them Moslems. Most of them farm the rich lands near the coast. Grain, grapes, and olives are the chief products. Tunisia also produces cork and pistachio nuts. The chief exports are olive oil and phosphates for fertilizer.

Tunisia was well known to the ancient world. The ruins of Carthage are near the present capital city of Tunis. During World War II, Tunisia was the site of many battles between Axis and Allied forces.

Libya has been called a "box of sand." Actually, it better deserves the name of "box of rocks," for nearly all of the country consists of rocky or pebbly desert.

Libya is nearly three times larger than Texas. Yet only slightly more than 1,000,-000 people live in this vast territory. Many of them are Bedouins—Arab nomads who wander from oasis to oasis raising flocks of sheep and goats.

There are three distinct regions in Libya. In the western portion of the country is *Tripolitania*, with its capital of Tripoli, a clean and modern city overlooking the Mediterranean.

Camels are more than "ships of the desert." A Libyan farmer yokes one to his primitive plow to farm his land.

Erich Kolmar—Shostal

On the sun-warmed slopes of a rocky Algerian hillside, an orange grove flourishes. Fruit is exported.

Tripoli was the scene of a stirring drama in early American history. On April 27, 1804, ships and Marines of the U.S. Navy successfully invaded the harbor, which was the base for the Barbary pirates who roamed the seas and plundered American ships. The Marines mark this battle in their Marine Hymn with the famous line, "From the halls of Montezuma to the shores of Tripoli." A major U.S. air base, Wheelus Field, is located near Tripoli.

Cyrenaica is the name of the eastern section of Libya. Its capital city is Benghazi. (Tripoli and Benghazi are considered co-capitals of the nation.) Benghazi is an ancient and poor city.

The third region is *The Fezzan*, a desert area south of Tripoli. The most important town in The Fezzan is Ghadamès, a stopover point on an ancient camel caravan route. Part of the city is built underground to escape the broiling heat of the desert.

Libya has been fought over by many countries ever since the Phoenicians founded colonies on the coast about 1,000 B.C. The Romans, the Greeks, the Vandals, the Arabs, the French, the Spanish, the Turks, and the Italians all controlled the country at one time or another.

Yet it is a desperately poor country. Except in tiny dots of cultivated land along the coastal rain belt, and a few desert oases, nothing can grow. One small section produces a few olives and figs. The rest is either scrubby pasture land or empty desert of no value.

The biggest and most important North African country is Algeria. Over nine tenths of its 846,000 square miles is desert, south of the Atlas Mountains. Most of the 10,000,000 people in the country live in the other one tenth.

That area is called Northern Algeria, and it is a rich and fertile land. The well-irrigated and terraced hills grow huge crops of wheat and barley. Colorful vineyards produce grapes that yield a heavy red wine. Olives, tobacco, fruits, vegetables, and dates are also grown in large quantities. The plateaus that stretch south toward the desert are also irrigated. This helps to increase the size of the cattle herds which are bred and pastured there.

Algeria was conquered by the Turks in 1518, but soon became a pirate nation ruled by anyone strong enough to seize and hold power. In 1830 the French invaded the country and took control.

H. Mensching

Because of long dry periods, water is precious. Algerian slopes are carefully irrigated and contour-plowed.

More than a million Europeans live in Northern Algeria. Most of them are Frenchmen. In the chief cities of Algiers (the capital), Oran, and Constantine, and in the farmlands just beyond the coast, French families have lived and worked for generations. But in recent years the Arabs have been fighting for the independence of the country. However, French settlers in Algeria have opposed independence for the country. They own most of the good land and control Algeria's economy. They fear what might happen if Algeria were free, for the Arabs outnumber them nine to one.

These feelings of intense nationalism are widespread in North Africa. After centuries in which their lands were ruled by outsiders, the native Arab peoples now want to control their own destinies.

White buildings cover the steep hills rising from the busy harbor of Algiers, Algeria's capital.

Philip D. Gendreau

Raymond Bricon

Against the backdrop of a colorful desert sunset, Bedouins lead their camels to the night's camp.

THE DESERT LANDS

The Arabic word "Sahara" means "emptiness." And the Sahara Desert is 3,500,000 square miles of emptiness. This immense area of sand and rock stretches from the Atlantic Ocean to the Red Sea, and cuts off North Africa from the bulk of the continent to the south.

Only a small part of the Sahara consists of sand dunes. These dunes shift constantly. This is the Great Erg, the most feared section of the desert. Most of the Sahara is made up of rock outcroppings, called *hamada*, and flat plains covered by boulders and gravel, called *reg*.

In the middle of the Sahara are huge mountain chains. The Ahaggar Mountains rise nearly two miles high from the desert. They were created by volcanic eruptions hundreds of thousands of years ago. Many of the peaks are extinct volcanoes.

An isolated village sits in the midst of the gravel desert that surrounds the Egyptian city of Thebes.

Paul F. Milhollan

Giant sand dunes cover the "Great Erg" region of the Sahara. Dunes are sculptured by prevailing winds.

Scientists once thought that the Sahara was the bed of an ancient, dried-up ocean. But today they believe it was formed by the "weathering" of the mountains. The heat of the day and the cold of the night, plus the constant winds and occasional fierce rainstorms and sandstorms, all combined to crack the rocks into smaller and smaller pieces until the particles were reduced to grains of sand. This process is still going on. Thousands of years from now the mountains of the Sahara will be worn away into sand.

Not all of the desert is bare. Much of the rocky part is covered by scraggly plant growth—coarse grass or stunted bushes. In certain places the underground water rises near enough to the surface for many desert plants to sink their long roots into it. These are the oases of the Sahara. In some places there is enough water so that the surrounding land can be cultivated and a life-giving well can be dug.

Some oases are merely a tiny clump of bushes and a trickle of water. Others have many springs and grow into towns of several thousand people. A typical oasis grows dates, citrus fruits, and vegetables.

Sometimes water is tapped sideways, rather than downwards. A channel dug horizontally into the base of higher land may strike underground water. The water then will flow down into the oasis by gravity. Such a channel is called a *foggara*.

Travelers in the desert move from oasis to oasis. Fifty years ago the only way to cross the Sahara was by camel. These beasts, called "ships of the desert," are uniquely equipped by nature to cope with the problems of desert life. The camel stores food in its hump and water in its stomach. In cool weather a camel can live for about two weeks without fresh water. In the summer, carrying men or goods, it must drink every other day. The camel is an awkward, ugly, bad-tempered animal. But it is the only one that can cross the great areas of shifting sand dunes.

Camel caravans sometimes number one hundred camels. The Arabs who lead the caravan are expert "navigators" of the desert. They guide themselves by remembering the size, shape, and location of the sand dunes and rocks, much as we can recall a route by its well-known landmarks.

But today it is also possible—although difficult and sometimes dangerous — to cross the Sahara by automobile. Travelers must notify the authorities of their route.

B. E. Lindroos—Gilloon

Dwellers of this date-palm oasis raise precious water from their well with a primitive sweep.

If they do not reach their destination within 24 hours, a rescue car is sent out to search for them. The major oases on the roads are from 200 to 300 miles apart. Any breakdown to a car can be dangerous. A person stranded in the desert without water in the summer can not live for much more than a day.

At a more flourishing Saharan oasis than the one above, springs yield enough water for irrigation canals.

Herbert Lanks—Shostal

Raymond Bricon

A caravan sets up tents near a "ksar"—an oasis village once fortified against Tuareg marauders.

Raymond Bricon

A camel train winds across the trackless Sahara. Caravan guides can memorize the routes.

Raymond Bricon

Tuareg men prepare their own tea by ritual.

Women of the Tuareg tribe spend much of their leisure time dressing each other's hair.

Raymond Bricon

Desert dwellers are of two main types. One type lives permanently at the oases. The other type roams the Sahara. Over the entire northern and western section of the Sahara the people are called Moors. They are of Arab origin, and are, for the most part, Moslems. Some of the nomadic Moors are known as Bedouins—wanderers of the desert.

In the southeastern part of the Sahara are a people called the Tibu, a word which means "rock people," for their home is in the rocky Tibesti Mountains, near the Sudan. They are of partly Negro stock.

Most fascinating of the peoples of the desert are the Tuareg. No one really knows where they came from. They are thought to be descendants of the Berbers who fled to the Sahara when the many waves of conquerors poured into North Africa. They are still a proud and independent people. The Tuareg are nomads. They wander over the desert, living in tents which are often made of leather. They raise goats, camels, and sheep.

In the rest of the Arab world the women wear veils over their faces. But among the Tuareg this custom is reversed. The faces of Tuareg women are uncovered, and those of the men are veiled. One explanation for this is that the Tuareg wanted to be different from other Arabs. But more probably the veil is simply a good means of protection from the desert sun.

Courtesy of TWA—Trans World Airlines

The three great Pyramids near Cairo rise from the desert sands. The green areas are Nile-irrigated fields.

Egypt, Land of the Nile

The greatest oasis in the Sahara is the Nile River valley—an oasis that is 700 miles long. Running the length of Egypt, it is the lifeline of the nation. The water that flows through it (from its sources deep in the rainforests of the Congo and high in Ethiopia) is Egypt's lifeblood.

It virtually never rains in Egypt. Over nine tenths of the country is desert. But once each year, in August and September, the Nile overflows its banks. These flood-waters have traveled several thousand miles from the rainy lands to the south. The muddy floodwaters flow over the valley lands, making them fertile.

The annual flooding of the Nile Valley has presented the rulers of Egypt with a

Hieroglyphics on the mighty Karnak Temple pillars tell the ancient stories of the Pharaohs.

Courtesy of TWA—Trans World Airlines

Shops in Egypt are open to the street, the better to attract possible buyers.

Bales of cotton are brought to a warehouse in Alexandria. Cotton is Egypt's chief export.

Egypt's growing population (about 29,-000,000) is expanding so fast that increased crop yields are not enough to support the nation's economy, despite flood control. Therefore, Egypt is developing industry. Many textile factories have been built to make cloth from Nile Valley cotton. Other growing industries are glass-ware, fertilizer, leather- and metal-working, and sugar refining.

Egypt's major port is the 2,300-year-old city of Alexandria, situated on the Nile Delta. Seven branches of the river flow through an immense triangle of sand. Lagoons and marshes cut off much of the land from the seacoast.

A vital part of Egypt's life is the Suez Canal. It is one of the most important waterways in the world. The Suez Canal cuts through the Arabian Desert to connect the Mediterranean and the Red Seas. Ships can go from Europe to Asia without making the long voyage around the tip of Africa. The Suez Canal was completed in 1869. It takes about 13 hours for a ship to make the 107-mile trip.

The Pyramids of Egypt rank among the wonders of the world. They were built by the ancient Pharaohs for their tombs. One of them, the Great Pyramid of Cheops, is constructed of 2,500,000 separate blocks of stone and is estimated to weigh nearly 5,000,000 tons. But today's Egyptians are more concerned with building new dams, factories, and ports for the future.

Egyptian worker operates a yarn drum in a Cairo textile mill. Industrialization is advancing rapidly.

The Suez Canal, vital to Europe's trade with the East, connects the Red and Mediterranean Seas.

The famous man-lion statue, the Sphinx, symbolizes Egypt's ancient past. It is nearly 5,000 years old.

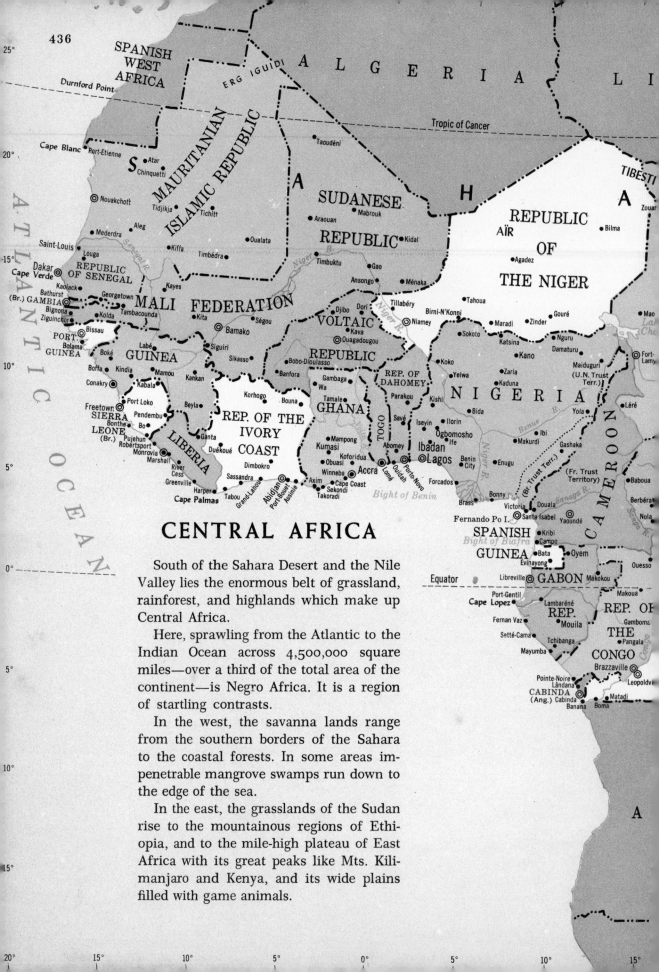

CENTRAL AFRICA

South of the Sahara Desert and the Nile Valley lies the enormous belt of grassland, rainforest, and highlands which make up Central Africa.

Here, sprawling from the Atlantic to the Indian Ocean across 4,500,000 square miles—over a third of the total area of the continent—is Negro Africa. It is a region of startling contrasts.

In the west, the savanna lands range from the southern borders of the Sahara to the coastal forests. In some areas impenetrable mangrove swamps run down to the edge of the sea.

In the east, the grasslands of the Sudan rise to the mountainous regions of Ethiopia, and to the mile-high plateau of East Africa with its great peaks like Mts. Kilimanjaro and Kenya, and its wide plains filled with game animals.

Boundaries of new republics within former French
Equatorial Africa and French West Africa may be
modified.

U. A. R.

(EGYPT)

RED SEA

GULF OF ADEN

BYA

MASSIF

• Aïn-Galaka

• Largeau

R

REPUBLIC

OF

CHAD

• Ati   • Abéché

• Melfi

• Am-Timan

• N'Délé

CENTRAL

atangafo • Fort-Crampel

Bossangoa   • Grimari

AFRICAN REP.

angui • Kouango

Zongo

• Monga • Ango

• Businga

Lisala • Bumba • Buta • Paulis

BELGIAN

Coquilhatville

Stanleyville

Stanley Falls

• Kirundu

• Monkoto

Lake Leopold II

Kutu

• Lomela

CONGO

• Kikwit • Luebo

• Feshi

OLA

• Kapanga

Lake Upemba

Sandoa

• Lubudi

Dilolo-Gare   • Kolwezi

• Jadotville

• Elisabethville

Sakania

Lake Nyasa

• Selima

Wadi Halfa

• Delgo

A

Muhammad Ghul

Port Sudan

• Dongola

Suakin

• Debba • Kareima • Berber   Aqiq

Atbara

• Shendi

Massawa

Omdurman

Khartoum

Keren   Mersa

Kassala   Asmara   Fatma

Umm Hajar

Wad Medani   Gedaref

Kosti

El Obeid   Roseires

• Geneina   • El Fasher   El Obeid

S U D A N

• Nyala   • Nahud   Gondar

Lake Tana

Debra
Markos

• Muglad   • Talodi

• Malakal

Belfodio

Makale

FR.
SOM.

Obock

Djibouti

Dikhil

Karin

Bulhar

Diredawa

Harar

Cape
Guardafui

Alula

Bender
Kassim

Berbera

Hargeisa

BRIT. SOM.

Bargal

Gardo

Bender Beila

Bohotieh

El Hamurre

Dabaro

ETHIOPIA

Addis Ababa

Saio

Gogrial   Nasir   Gore

• Wau   • Tonj   Akobo

Jimma

Soddu

Ginir

Gorrahei

S O M A L I A

Wardere

Shebeli R.

Harar-
dera

Mongalla

• Maji

Alga

Yambio   Juba   Torit

• Negelli

Dolo

Meregh

Isha
Baidoa

Mega

Mandera

Itala

Mogadishu

Merca

CENTRAL

Bomu R.

Uele R.

Lake Albert

Kitgum

Lake Rudolf

Marsabit

Wajir

Brava

Afmadu

Muddo Gashi

Gelib

Masindi
(Br.)   Soroti

UGANDA   KENYA

Fort Portal

Entebbe   Kampala   Kisumu   Nakuru
(Br.)

Kabale

Lake Edward

Lake Kivu

RUANDA-
URUNDI

Astrida

Usumbura

Rutana

Fizi

Lake Victoria

Naivasha

Nairobi

Ngong

Bura

Witu

Lamu

Malindi

Takaungu

Mombasa

Mwanza

Arusha

Moshi

(Br. Trust
Territory)

Tabora

Kondoa

Ujiji   Dodoma   Mpwapwa

Lake Tanganyika

Karema

TANGANYIKA

Kabalo

Moba

Iringa

Manono

Pweto

Kasanga   Chunya

Mbeya

Manda

Mwaya

Tunduru

Masasi

Newala

Pemba

ZANZIBAR (Br. Prot.)

Zanzibar

Dar es Salaam

INDIAN

OCEAN

Mohoro

Kilwa

Lindi

Cape Delgado

40°   45°   50°

FEDERATION OF

RHODESIA

AND

NYASALAND

20°   25°   30°   35°

CENTRAL AFRICA

0 _____ 500
Miles

◉ National Capitals
◎ Other Capitals

Addis Ababa _____ 250,000-1,000,000 population
Constantine _____ 100,000- 250,000 population
Katsina _____ 50,000- 100,000 population
El Fasher _____ Under 50,000 population

© Copyright 1960 by Map Projects Inc.

Charles Trieschmann—Camera Clix

A dense growth of head-high grasses with scattered bushes and trees is typical of savanna landscapes.

Dugout canoes serve as a ferry for natives crossing a crocodile-infested river in Nigeria.

Charles Trieschmann—Camera Clix

Between these regions lie the central equatorial plateau and the immense basin of the Congo. This is wet, hot rainforest.

Central Africa is the land of tribal chiefs and witch doctors, of the tsetse fly and the malaria-carrying mosquito. But here, too, modern cities are being built not far from where near-naked tribesmen still live in thatch-roofed huts in the jungle.

This is a land of tremendous untapped riches in the form of natural resources. It is a land where native Africans are eager to govern themselves. Although many of the countries in Central Africa are still under the control of European nations, others have recently won their independence or are on the verge of doing so.

The massive Congo river flows sluggishly through the rainforest, reaching out its watery fingers in hundreds of tributaries to drain 1,600,000 square miles of the Central African plateau.

The savanna lands of Central Africa form about a 700-mile-wide belt of grassland, scattered trees and shrubs, and rolling plateau. Part of it is used for farming or for cattle grazing. The tall-grass plains of the eastern region are big game country. Hunters go there on safari to shoot lion, elephant, rhinoceros, and other animals.

The cattle herders live for the most part in the northern section of this belt, where the short grass makes good pasture land for their herds. Most famous of the cattle-raisers are the Masai, a tall and proud tribe living in East Africa. They have little to do with civilization, refusing to grow crops or to learn skilled work. They do not eat meat, but live on the milk of their cattle.

Cattle-raising areas are sharply restricted by the presence of the tsetse fly. Thousands of head of cattle have been wiped out by it. In recent years, however, some progress has been made in clearing certain regions of the tsetse fly by spraying poisonous chemicals, and by making sure infected cattle do not enter the cleared territory.

B. E. Lindroos—Gilloon

Dense rainforest borders the Ogooué River in the French Cameroons, scene of Dr. Schweitzer's work.

Ornamented Samburu tribeswoman trains her child to guard native sheep on the Kenya plains.

Hans von Meiss—Photo Researchers

Charles May—Shostal

Citizens of Accra, in Ghana, line up for rations of water when dry season cuts normal supply.

Stutts—Rapho Guillumette

Native women sell their wares in a new covered concrete marketplace in Abidjan, Ivory Coast.

Huge "dunce-cap" thatches serve as hut roofs in a typical Liberian village scene.

Alfred Zulliger—Shostal

Life in West Africa

Perhaps the most exciting region of Africa today is West Africa, where great strides toward political and economic independence are being taken. In the rush of progress, the old and the new provide striking contrasts—tin-roofed huts stand next to modern office buildings, and African taxi drivers dressed in colorful native robes steer their cabs through traffic.

West Africa was the home of great Negro empires nearly 1,000 years ago. The first of them was Ghana, which flourished around 1,000 A.D. Its capital was the desert city of Ghana, about 250 miles west of Timbuktu. Other Negro empires which, in their turn, ruled the savanna lands were the Mandingo, the Songhai, and the Fulani.

West Africa stretches from Cape Verde in the east to the mountains of the Cameroons in the west; from the edge of the Sahara in the north to the swampy coast of the Gulf of Guinea in the south. Its chief rivers are the Niger and the Volta.

By and large, West Africans are a happy and friendly people. The men are tall and handsome. The women dress in gaily colored cotton clothes and turbans that make them look like Arabian Nights princesses. Most of the men nowadays wear western clothes except in Ghana, where the native costume is still proudly worn.

The waters of the Gulf of Guinea are rough. In addition, the land slopes very gradually away from shore for about half a mile, then drops suddenly to great depths. As a result, cargo ships find it difficult to unload their goods. Few countries have as yet built sheltered harbors, but Ghana is building such a port at Tema, about 20 miles from its capital, Accra.

One of the most exciting sights in Africa is the boatmen at Accra going out to unload the big vessels that stand offshore. The paddlers, stripped to the waist, push off in their huge, canoe-shaped boats. They ply their painted, three-bladed paddles

New and old in Ghana: left, modern Supreme Court buildings; right, fishermen's painted canoes

with all their strength. The canoes are lifted high by one huge roller, then dropped breathtakingly into the trough of the next. Cargo is transferred from the ship to the canoe, the paddlers turn the boat around and head for shore, timing their paddle thrusts to the swell of the waves. Once through the surf some paddlers jump overboard and guide the canoe to the beach. There other Ghanaians wade into the breakers, lift the cargo to their heads, and carry it over the sand and rocks to warehouses that line the beachfront. All kinds of goods, from sacks of food to grand pianos, have been unloaded this way. But it is not unusual to see a canoe upset by a huge roller, and its cargo and its paddlers tossed into the sea.

Canoes and muscular paddlers brave heavy surf at Accra to unload cargo from off-shore vessels.

A cacao grower inspects the pods on one of his trees to see whether they are ready to harvest.

Hides from animals like these sheep grazing on the Jos Plateau are one of Nigeria's major exports.

Resources of the Savanna Lands

The crops of the West African Guinea Coast are rich and varied. They range from peanuts and kola nuts to cassava and corn, from palm oil and bananas to coffee and cacao. Rice grows well in some of the swampy coastal regions, such as those in Liberia, Sierra Leone, and Gambia. The chief crop of Ghana is cacao.

The cacao plants are grown on small farms rather than large plantations. Yet despite this, Ghana produces more than two thirds of the world's supply of cacao.

Logs of valuable tropical wood float in a Ghana harbor awaiting transport to lumber mill.

Workmen in Senegal pile up a huge mound of peanuts for shipment. Peanuts are Senegal's chief crop.

The biggest threat to a cacao farmer is swollen shoot, a plant disease carried by mealybugs. It once threatened to wipe out the whole industry before it was brought under control.

In the eastern savanna lands of the Sudan, hunting and herding are combined with the growing of grains and cotton. A 1,000,000-acre area called the Gezira, in southern Sudan, was once a flat plain that received little rainfall. Co-operation between government agencies, private enterprise, and Sudanese farmers developed a massive irrigation scheme. Today the Gezira gets a steady supply of water from a dam on the Nile. Thousands of acres of land have been brought under cultivation as a result.

An unusual area in the Sudan is the Sudd—a vast marshland along the Nile filled with masses of floating vegetation. There are many fish in the Sudd. Sudanese natives spear them and dry them for a year-round food supply. The Sudd also has great areas of papyrus grass.

The Central African savanna, in addition to being good farming and grazing land, holds the promise of widespread mineral resources. Although the lack of roads has prevented much exploration, some geologists believe the area will prove rich in various ores.

Diamonds, almost entirely for industrial use, are still produced in Sierra Leone and in Ghana. The latter country (formerly known as the Gold Coast) also has gold-bearing ore. But most natural resources today are in strategic rather than in the so-called "precious" metals: manganese in French West Africa; iron ore in Sierra Leone; manganese and bauxite, the basic source of aluminum, in Ghana, where large-scale mining is being developed; and tin (nearly one quarter of the world's supply) and coal in Nigeria.

Nigerian tin miners work with primitive tools to extract this valuable mineral resource.

Shostal

Two Sudanese scoop up cotton as a third bales it. The Gezira is a cotton-rich region of the Sudan.

Stutts—Rapho Guillumette

Above: modern machinery stockpiles iron ore on the loading docks of Liberia.

Stephanie Dinkins—FLO

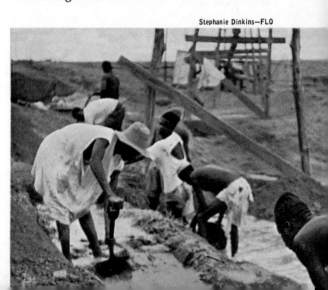

Charles Trieschmann—Camera Clix

Tallest smokestack in Africa dominates 20-story slag-heap of copper smelter in Elisabethville.

Wayne Fredericks—House of Photography

Modern buildings line the streets of Léopoldville, capital city of the Belgian Congo.

Martin Simpson—Annan Photo Features

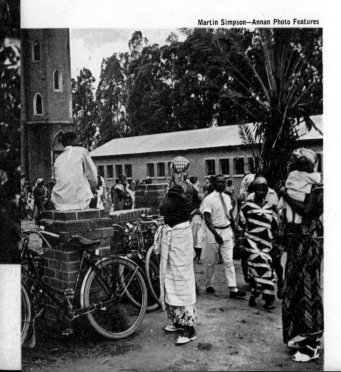

The vast extent and wealth of the Congo were first realized by the explorer Henry Stanley. His plan to develop the area was supported by King Leopold II of Belgium. In its early days, the Congo was valuable for such resources as rubber, ivory, and oil palms. But when engineers pushed railroads through to the Katanga, an area in the southeastern part of the Congo Basin, mining became the base of the Congo's wealth.

Diamonds and gold are found in sizable amounts in the eastern uplands of the Congo. But they cannot compare in value to the riches of the Katanga. Here is one of the greatest mineral-bearing tracts in the world. Its chief ore is copper. Huge open-pit mines yield millions of tons.

The Katanga is also rich in tin and zinc. It has more cobalt than any area in the world, and it is a major producer of uranium from heavily guarded mines at Shinkolobwe. Uranium from the Congo was used to make America's first atomic bomb. Other minerals of the Congo include manganese, platinum ores, tungsten, and coal.

The mineral wealth of the Belgian Congo has made it a prosperous country. Léopoldville is much like a medium-sized American city. It has broad streets, ten-story skyscrapers, apartment houses, factories, and warehouses along the Congo River. The chief city of the Katanga district is Elisabethville, also a bustling modern community.

Huge plants, filled with complicated machinery, process the Katanga ores. African workers operate and supervise many of the machines. They live in nearby communities of neat houses, each with its small garden.

Yet not far away in the rainforest other Africans live in primitive tribal ways.

Their homes are small round huts made of baked mud, with peaked roofs of straw or mud. They have no floors or windows.

Churchgoers arrive by bicycle at Sunday services of Elisabethville Church of Christ of the Congo.

Some tribes eat only one meal a day. The food is mostly palm oil, corn, and cereal. Occasionally there is meat from a monkey killed by a hunter's spear or arrow.

The men and women tattoo their skins, or make knife cuts in special patterns so the scars will form designs. They paint their skin with dyes, and talk through the forest by pounding out signals on huge wooden drums.

Also a part of Equatorial Africa's rainforest region is the southern half of the former region of French Equatorial Africa. The country has 1,000,000 square miles, making it almost four times as large as Texas. This vast area spreads from the Congo River and the Atlantic Ocean 1,500 miles north to the edges of the Sahara Desert. Its capital, Brazzaville, is on the Congo opposite Léopoldville.

French Equatorial Africa has no large cities. Transportation is primitive and difficult. Tropical woods, wild rubber, and palm oil are the major resources of the southern rainforest region. Although the land is still undeveloped, there are indications that great mineral wealth lies untapped there.

Courtesy of the Belgian Congo Tourist Bureau

Above: Congo village huts are shaded by palm tree. Below: Congo youngster helps with chores.

Martin Simpson—Annan Photo Features

A group of men drive animals laden with sacks of grain down a flooded road in French Equatorial Africa.

Charles Trieschmann—Camera Clix

Hans von Meiss—Photo Researchers

Ethiopian villagers check condition of beeswax hardening in molds. Beeswax is exported.

Martin Simpson—Annan Photo Features

Ethiopian tribesmen haul water from well in goat-skin bucket for herd of thirsty cattle.

The Eastern Highlands

The savanna lands end abruptly at a mountain barrier that forms the highlands of Ethiopia. This country, ruled by an emperor, is a rugged land with a history going back thousands of years. Legend has it that Ethiopia was once ruled by the Queen of Sheba.

Ethiopia's volcanic mountains tower to 13,000 feet. At the higher altitudes, cattle, sheep, and goats are raised. Lower on the slopes, grain, sugar cane, cotton, coffee, dates, figs, and citrus fruits are grown. In the drier plains, gum, beeswax, and the Biblical herbs of frankincense and myrrh are produced.

Still farther east the land drops swiftly to the Red Sea and the Indian Ocean. Most of the coastal lands are desert.

South of Ethiopia, the East African plateau rises sharply from the coast. It is separated from the Central African plateau on the west by a gigantic rift valley with

Rich farmlands lie part fallow, part cultivated beneath the ramparts of an Ethiopian mountain range.

Bernheim-Conant, AMNH—FLO

Washday is a busy time at this public laundry in Mombasa. Use of the tubs is free to the public.

chains of long, narrow, deep lakes. It is a region of high plains and mountains. The area is often called British East Africa.

This region, especially Kenya, is a favorite of white settlers in Africa. The reason is that much of the area is a mile or more above sea level. Thus, even though Kenya's highlands are squarely on the equator, the climate is more comfortable than in the tropical lowlands. Temperatures range from about 80 degrees during the day to as low as 35 degrees at night.

The northern half of Kenya, which is a British colony, is semi-desert. The coastal strip and its chief port, Mombasa, are hot and humid. Nairobi, the mile-high capital, is in the central plateau. It is a modern, busy city, and the hub of trade and transportation for the region.

Most of the European settlers live in the Kenya highlands, a region of good farmland. They grow coffee, tea, sisal, corn, and wheat. The native Kikuyu tribesmen are crowded into a smaller area, with less good land. This led to a native rebellion. The rebels called themselves Mau Maus. The rebellion was put down, but the natives' feelings still run high against the white settlers and government.

Nairobi, the capital of Kenya, is the largest European settlement in East Africa. Nairobi is famous as the "safari capital" of Africa.

Alfred G. Milotte

Thousands of animals gather at a waterhole in the Serengeti Plains, famous game region.

An isolated native village with thatch-roofed huts stands in Kenya's acacia-dotted savanna lands.

Martin Simpson—Annan Photo Features

These long-horned Kenya cattle are about to be sprayed against disease-carrying insects.

Richard Harrington—Annan Photo Features

A Moslem in Tanganyika weaves a straw sleeping mat. Mats like these are popular with tourists.

Nairobi is the safari capital of Africa. There are six national parks and six game reserves in Kenya. One, the 8,000-square-mile Tsavo reserve, is especially for elephants. South from Nairobi, but across the border into Tanganyika, are the famous Serengeti Plains, where hunters try their skill and luck against Africa's most spectacular assortment of wild animals.

Tanganyika is a British-administered United Nations trust territory. Much of it is dry. Large areas are covered by scrub and grassland. Farming is poor except in the region surrounding Mt. Kilimanjaro. This is the center of the rainfall area. The rain that falls on the mountain's slopes runs down to streams and lakes in the neighboring country, providing enough water for farming. The main crop is sisal, which thrives on poor, dry soils. Coffee and cotton are also successfully grown.

Land-locked Uganda is a bridge from the northern savanna lands to equatorial Africa. In the north, Uganda's swamps

Safari Productions—Photo Researchers

merge with those of Sudan. In the south, it borders the Congo rainforest. It is a fertile and prosperous British territory. The main crop is cotton, but tobacco, tea, coffee, and sugar also grow there.

Moshi Mosque in Tanganyika is a religious center for Moslems. In background is Mt. Kilimanjaro.

Hans von Meiss—Photo Researchers

A family in a Uganda village spreads out coffee to dry before shipping it to market.

Tea is a major product of Uganda. These carefully tended tea trees are part of a plantation.

Lake Victoria is a huge, shallow body of water surrounded by Kenya, Uganda, and Tanganyika. It is one of a chain of lakes running north and south through British East Africa along the line of the Great Rift Valley. The others are Lakes Rudolf, Albert, Edward, Tanganyika, and Nyasa.

Lake Victoria is the second largest body of fresh water in the world (Lake Superior is the biggest). Yet its greatest depth is only 250 feet. It is infested with crocodiles and hippos and the organism of bilharziasis. The lake is important as the source of the Nile. A new dam at Owen Falls helps to control the Nile's waters and provides hydroelectric power for Uganda. Eventually the dam may be able to bring cheap power to much of the Congo region.

Instead of nets, these fishermen use a circle of woven papyrus to catch fish in a Uganda lake.

Above: Arab sailors tend their *dhow* on the waterfront of Zanzibar, an ancient port city.

Above right: clove trees blossom on a commercial plantation. Cloves are Zanzibar's chief crop.

Center: the narrow, winding streets and Arab-style houses of Zanzibar resemble those of North Africa.

Zanzibar, the Isle of Cloves

Twenty miles off the British East African coast lies the island of Zanzibar. It is ruled by a nominally independent sultan who is, however, under a British protectorate.

Zanzibar is an Arab community. It used to be a center of activity for Arab slave traders. Today, Zanzibar and its sister island of Pemba grow and export most of the world's clove supply. (Cloves are the dried flower buds of a small tree.)

The dhow—the wide-sailed vessel used so much on the Nile River in Egypt—is a common sight in Zanzibar's harbor. Arab seamen sail their dhows to India and back, using the seasonal monsoon winds, which blow steadily in one direction. The trip takes about two weeks.

Right: native shoppers examine the wares of this open-air grocery. The veiled woman is a Moslem.

Rocky coastline and jutting headlands thrust out into the waters of Pringle Bay, South Africa.

SOUTHERN AFRICA

The narrow southern third of the continent of Africa is vastly different from the northern and central sections. A belt of savanna land—not so wide as the one in the north—forms a transition zone between the Congo rainforests and the deserts of South-West Africa and Bechuanaland. These deserts are small compared with the Sahara.

At the southern tip of the continent we are no longer in the tropics. The Union of South Africa lies almost entirely south of the Tropic of Capricorn. Here the seasons are reversed when compared with those of countries north of the equator. Summer starts in December, and winter begins in July.

These lands were climatically attractive to white settlers. The Portuguese, Dutch, and British founded colonies there.

Southern Africa is a varied region. The Rhodesias are a great mining center. The Union of South Africa has rich grazing and farming lands wherever water is available, and on the coast are industrial cities and seaside resorts.

Racial tensions are greater in southern Africa than anywhere else in the continent. The white minority has enforced rigid segregation of the Negroes, and keeps strict control over their employment and private lives. *Apartheid*, an attempt to separate by law the white and African communities, is the policy of the Union of South Africa.

Horse and rider pause to view the majesty of 630-foot Maletsunyane Falls, in Basutoland, South Africa.

Fishing, picnicking, and painting are popular activities at the South African resort of Knysna.

The Union of South Africa

The Union of South Africa covers 472,-000 square miles. This makes it almost twice the size of the state of Texas. It is the dominant nation, both politically and economically, in southern Africa.

The Union is an independent nation. Of its 13,000,000 people, about four fifths are Bantu Negroes. The white inhabitants are thus in a four-to-one minority. Even this minority is split between British and Afrikaners, who are mostly descendants of early Dutch settlers. They are called "Afrikaners" because they speak a language called "Afrikaans," a South African tongue derived from Dutch but with many African words added to it. There are also more than 1,000,000 Coloreds (people of mixed blood) and 500,000 Asians (mostly Indians) in the Union.

Rich Transvaal farmland has varied landscape— flowering trees, rocky crags, level grasslands.

The Afrikaners control the national government. But of the four provinces that make up the Union, two are dominated by the British (Cape and Natal) and two by the Afrikaners (Transvaal and Orange Free State).

All of southern Africa roughly follows this geographical pattern: there is a high central plateau bounded by mountains in the east and dry lands toward the west. Hills and valleys alternate in huge "steps" as the land drops to the seacoasts. Most of the Union gets little rainfall. When rain does come, it often falls in the form of heavy storms that wash away the soil. The few rivers are usually either flooded or dry. In some areas dams provide water for irrigation; elsewhere there are deep wells.

A Zulu youth wanders the grass-covered hillsides of Natal Province with his burros.

South Africa exports large quantities of fruit. This pineapple field is in Natal Province.

Martin Simpson—Annan Photo Features

Cape and Natal Provinces are the coastal regions of the Union of South Africa. They are the most scenic and fertile.

The coastal provinces were the first areas settled by Europeans. The Portuguese landed there as long ago as 1482. When it was realized that whoever controlled the

Cape of Good Hope was master of the sea route from Europe to India, the Dutch and English also colonized the Cape. The only African tribes there then were primitive Bushmen and Hottentots.

Cape Province has magnificent scenery. In the interior, river valleys curve through mountains which are carpeted with wild flowers in the South African spring. Fruit orchards and vineyards nestle in the valleys. On the coast, modern cities ring curving ocean beaches. The strong-surf mingles the waters of the Indian and Atlantic oceans.

The capital city is Cape Town, which sits at the foot of flat-topped Table Mountain. A scenic drive leads to the tip of Africa, the Cape of Good Hope.

Wheat is the principal crop of Cape Province, but most of the soil produces delicious fruits, especially plums and apples. The vines yield grapes which make excellent wine.

Negroes labor in the vineyard tending grapevines. South Africa produces excellent red and white wines.

Gordon Douglas—FPG

Rupert Leach—Shostal

Martin S. Klein

Above: more than half a million people live in Durban, South Africa's chief port.

Above right: thousands enjoy sand, sun, and surf on Durban's beaches. Summer there is December to February.

Right: Zulu ricksha "boys" dress in colorful tribal costumes to attract riders for their carts in Durban.

Wayne Fredericks—House of Photography

Natal is called the "Garden Province" of the Union. This province gets a considerable amount of rainfall and grows citrus fruits, bananas, pineapple, and pawpaws. Its chief crop is sugar cane. Natal's capital city is Pietermaritzburg. But its most important city is Durban, the principal seaport for the entire Union.

Durban exports large quantities of coal, as well as gold and other mineral wealth produced in the interior of the country. Its sandy beaches are excellent for swimming. Durban is the most popular resort in the Union. Visitors can ride in rickshas (two-wheeled carriages) drawn by Zulu tribesmen dressed in colorful beads and feathers. Visitors can also tour a nearby game reserve famous for its rare white rhinoceroses.

Most of the Indian population of the Union is concentrated in Durban and other coastal areas of Natal.

An Indian woman of Natal poses with her children. Most Natal Indians are shopkeepers or gardeners.

John and Bini Moss—Photo Researchers

Elizabeth Morton—American Museum of Natural History

Rolling fields of the Transkei are used for grain crops and stock raising. Many mine workers come from here.

Back of the mountains that separate the eastern coast of South Africa from the central plateau is the *veld*. The veld is rolling grassland, like the savanna of Central Africa. Depending on the altitude and the amount of rainfall, the veld is used for farming or for grazing. Corn and wheat are the chief crops. Immense sheep ranches breed Merino sheep, famous for their silky wool.

The veld lies largely in the two Afrikaner-dominated provinces — Transvaal and Orange Free State. These two provinces were created as a result of the "Great Trek," a milestone in South Africa's history. It began in 1836, when the pressure of British colonists in the coast regions began forcing the Dutch farmers (called Boers) into the interior.

Helen Joy Lee—FPG

African women work from dawn to dusk in the fields of a South African soybean plantation.

Corn, called "mealies," is a staple of the African diet. This woman husks corn to grind the kernels.

Boer farmers hitched 16 oxen to huge covered wagons and set out across the great grassy plains. They faced thirst and starvation, attacks by hostile Zulus and other warrior tribes, and months of loneliness. But they grimly plodded on, across the Vaal River, and founded the two new provinces.

Isolated in the high up-country, the Boers became more independent and more anti-British. Their frequent battles with the Negro tribes fed their fear and hatred of the Africans.

A typical veld farm in the Orange Free State is a lonely place. Millions of sheep are pastured on the grasslands. In the lower veld of the Transvaal, grazing gives way to farming, and there are important citrus farms. About one third of the Transvaal is covered by the treeless, grassy High Veld, but most of it is "bushveld," with scattered shrubs dotting the flatlands that lie between range after range of low hills. The Transvaal's farms produce cotton, to-

John and Bini Moss—Photo Researchers

bacco, and peanuts. Fruit orchards and cattle ranches also add to the region's wealth. Wool, hides, and skins are important exports.

Cattle graze on the treeless plains of the High Veld, over 6,000 feet high.

H. E. Street—Shostal

Gordon Douglas—FPG

Government buildings in Pretoria, South Africa's capital, frame the statue of Boer hero Louis Botha.

Transvaal Province is the center of the Union's mining industry. Besides the world-famous Johannesburg gold mines, its resources include coal, diamonds, asbestos, platinum, chromium, and copper. There are important deposits of iron ore northwest of Pretoria. There are huge blast furnaces and steel mills at Pretoria and Vanderbijl Park, near Vereeniging. The Union of South Africa produces nearly enough steel to satisfy its needs.

Pretoria is the capital city of Transvaal and the headquarters of the government of the Union. But the main city of the Transvaal, as well as of the Union of South Africa, is Johannesburg.

Ndebele tribesmen, who live in villages near Pretoria, are famed for their magnificent decorative work.

Hans von Meiss—Photo Researchers

H. E. Street—Shostal

Town Hall Square provides a fine open space in the center of Johannesburg's downtown business section.

Kruger National Park is the most famous of all African game preserves. It is nearly the size of Massachusetts—certainly the biggest zoo in the world. Driving along its 1,500 miles of roads one can see lions, leopards, elephants, giraffes, zebras, crocodiles, baboons, and many other animals. The park is named after Paul Kruger, who was for many years president of the Transvaal.

A sable antelope forages at sunset on the open plains of Kruger National Park in South Africa.

M. M. Schechter

A lazy lioness rests at the side of a road in Kruger National Park. Visitors must stay in their cars.

M. M. Schechter

Johannesburg's fabulous gold mines, with their huge dumps of debris, create a striking backdrop for the city.

Miner hauls ore cart through underground tunnel.

Southern Africa's Mineral Wealth

Southern Africa is a storehouse of mineral wealth. The gold produced by the Union of South Africa amounts to nearly half of the total world output. Its diamond mines yield fortunes in fabulous gems. It is rich, too, in uranium, maganese, chrome, lead, and coal. Farther north, in the Federation of Rhodesia and Nyasaland, are huge deposits of copper, mica, chrome, and asbestos.

The discovery of gold in South Africa created Johannesburg, Africa's third largest city. Today 1,000,000 people live there. Half of this total are whites, many of them mine owners and businessmen. Half are Negroes imported to work the mines or to be domestic servants.

Johannesburg sits on the crest of the "Witwatersrand," a 100-mile-long vein of gold-bearing ore. Mine shafts and tunnels

These neat "compound" houses shelter workers imported to labor in the Johannesburg gold mines.

run thousands of feet deep underneath the city. On Johannesburg's outskirts are great mounds of rock and soil, waste material from the mining operations.

Africans in Johannesburg, as in other major Union cities, live in a "location"—a kind of slum on the outskirts of town. Thousands of Negroes live cramped in tiny shacks built of bits of wood or metal or other scrap. Most of the conveniences of living — bathrooms, lighting, telephones, and transportation—are not available in the locations.

Several hundred thousand African men who work in the Rand gold mines live in compounds outside Johannesburg. The compounds are housing areas set aside for the Africans by the mine operators. These workers are Bantus, many of whom come from neighboring countries. One of the

Martin S. Klein

famous sights of Johannesburg is the mine dances held on Sundays in the compounds. Young men from scores of different tribes do their tribal dances in stadiums before enthusiastic audiences.

Mine workers forget daily toil in the excitement of tribal dances. Teams compete before packed stands.

Martin S. Klein

Water slowly fills one of the great diamond mines discovered at Kimberley, world's diamond capital.

A fortune in gems is held in these hands. But synthetic diamond manufacture may cut their value.

Diamonds were first discovered in South Africa on the Orange River. The outstanding diamond mine was found at Kimberley, in Cape Province. The mine there is called the "Big Hole." It is three quarters of a mile wide and nearly one third of a mile deep—one of the largest man-made holes on earth. Millions of dollars worth of diamonds have been mined from it.

Diamonds are measured in carats. A carat is two tenths of a gram—a tiny fraction of an ounce. But their value also depends on their color (blue-white is the best) and the skill with which they are cut into gems.

The biggest diamond ever found was the Cullinan diamond, which came from a mine near Pretoria. It was the size of a man's fist. Diamond mining, as well as gold mining, is monopolized by huge firms that control mining, distribution, and sales.

In the southwest, near the mouth of the Orange River, other diamond fields occur. It is possible to spot diamonds lying in the sand deserts or on the beaches. But if you find one you cannot keep it. The area is closely guarded. Even visitors are searched when they leave the area.

The mining areas of southern Africa extend northward from the Union into the Rhodesias and Nyasaland. Rhodesia is named after Cecil Rhodes, a British millionaire and adventurer who was a major figure in the development of British Africa.

Much of Northern and Southern Rhodesia is a great expanse of savanna land. In Southern Rhodesia cattle ranching is done on the grassy plateau. Citrus fruits, corn, and tobacco grow. Teak and mahogany forests in the lowlands provide lumber for the sawmills. The coal fields at Wankie produce 2,000,000 tons a year—not nearly enough to meet the needs of an area that is rapidly growing more and more industrialized. In Salisbury, the capital, and Bulawayo, the chief rail center, textile mills and machine tool plants are busy. In Northern Rhodesia the rich copper veins of the Katanga region are mined.

The boundary between the Rhodesias is formed largely by the Zambezi River. The town of Livingstone, named for the famous explorer, is right on the border at Victoria Falls. Where the Zambezi runs through a narrow gorge near Kariba, in Southern Rhodesia, a huge dam will provide power and water for millions of acres of this still largely undeveloped territory.

Nyasaland is a finger-shaped region. Most of the population are natives. Nyasa-

A huge steam shovel looks like a toy as it digs ore from an open-pit copper mine in Northern Rhodesia.

land is potentially rich farm country. Tea and tobacco are raised in the highlands. Nyasaland and the two Rhodesias were recently formed into the Federation of Rhodesia and Nyasaland. But the fact that there are a large number of whites in Southern Rhodesia, and an overwhelming majority of Negroes in the other two divisions, is leading to arguments about segregation and other political problems.

Kariba Dam on the Zambezi River in Rhodesia will form the world's largest man-made lake.

This is typical housing for Africans in Angola.

Lourenço Marques is a leading African port.

Colonial Lands and Native Reserves

To the east and west of the Federation are the two huge Portuguese territories in Africa. On the east is Mozambique, on the west, Angola. Both are almost completely undeveloped.

Angola has 4,000,000 people in its 481,000 square miles. Cattle are raised in the savanna lands, and peanuts, cassava, rice, and corn are grown.

Mozambique has 5,000,000 people in 298,000 square miles. Cotton, sisal, and copra are the chief crops. But the colony's importance rests on its port and capital, Lourenço Marques. From there, some of Rhodesia's and South Africa's exports are shipped to foreign markets.

South-West Africa is a dry plateau which falls sharply to the sea. Much of it is actual desert. Part of the Kalahari Desert extends into it. There are about 400,000 people in South-West Africa, almost all Africans. Sheep, goat, and karakul sheep ranches dot the desolate countryside. Some metals—tin, lead, copper, and zinc—are

A common sight on the South African veld are the windmills which pump water for livestock and farming.

M. M. Schechter

Groups of fenced huts make up the village of Kanye, Bechuanaland, on the edge of the Kalahari Desert.

worked in the northern reaches of the country. There are important diamond fields along the coast.

South-West Africa is administered by the Union of South Africa and sends representatives to the Union government. But it is also a trust territory of the United Nations.

Southern Africa has three areas of land set aside as native reserves. The largest of these is Bechuanaland, between Southern Rhodesia and the Union of South Africa. It is a British protectorate, as big as Texas. But only about 3,000,000 Bantu tribespeople live there. The southern part of the country is in the Kalahari Desert. The northern part is swampland.

The two other native reserves are enclaves—small areas of land entirely surrounded by the Union of South Africa, but under British administration. They are Swaziland and Basutoland. They are more

thickly populated than Bechuanaland, but the land is poor. The tribes live in *kraals*, or villages, and follow traditional ways of life. They raise cattle and live near their herds in small round huts called *rondavels*. Most of the young men in the reserves seek work in the mines and cities of South Africa rather than stay on the reserve.

Courtesy of the South African Tourist Corporation

African women pound cassava roots in huge tubs to make a pasty meal which is their main food.

South African tribesmen are proud of their long-horned cattle, which they regard as a sign of wealth.

The story of the origin of Basutoland is like an exciting novel. In 1820, Bantu tribes from Central Africa were rushing southward, killing or enslaving any tribes which did not flee. One warrior, Moshesh, formed the refugees into rough troops and hid out in the mountains. He and his men fought the Bantu invaders to a standstill.

Isolated in their mountain country, the people of Basutoland suffer many handicaps. They have no real political freedom. Their country is poor. And superstition has flourished, so that witch doctors still wield great power.

In Bechuanaland, African families wait patiently in long lines for X-ray examinations in a lab on wheels.

Youngsters gather around the community pump in a Bechuanaland village. Behind them is a clinic.

The dry lands in the western half of Southern Africa are very limited in their usefulness. One such area is the Karroo, which is a region of treeless plains hemmed in by mountains in the northern part of Cape Province.

In a few places irrigation makes it possible to grow wheat, tobacco, and grapes. But over most of the Karroo the only vegetation is stunted shrubs. Yet these bushes provide pasture for large herds of Merino sheep and for goats.

Farther north and west, where it may rain only once in two or three years, the Upper Karroo region is the center of karakul sheep ranching country.

Fat-tailed Persian sheep can be bred to yield two different kinds of fur. One comes in tight curls and is known as "Persian lamb." The other is flat, smooth, and sleek. It is called "karakul."

M. M. Schechter

Both karakul and Persian lambs live short lives. When a lamb is about four days old its fur begins to lose the tight curls of Persian lamb or the luxuriousness of karakul; so it is killed to preserve the quality of its fur. The best lambs are saved for breeding purposes.

A brief shower of rain can turn the drab, sun-baked Karroo into a carpet of flowering plants.

Dan Weiner—Rapho

THE FUTURE OF AFRICA

Today, Africa and its people are on the threshold of a new life. A continent that was virtually unknown barely 100 years ago is now plunged into the midst of Western civilization.

Not long ago the chief of a Uganda tribe used to kill his enemies by tossing them to crocodiles in a lake. Now the grandson of that chief, a graduate of a British university, uses the lake as a swimming pool for himself and his friends.

Nowhere in the world have so many things changed so quickly for so many people. For example, until the white man came, African Negroes never knew of the use of the wheel, one of mankind's earliest and most important discoveries. (A wheel went on a cart or a wagon, which was pulled by animals. And domestic animals could not live where the tsetse fly lived.)

Yet today millions of Africans own bicycles. A few own automobiles, and many have learned to drive tractors and locomotives.

Africans whose fathers lived in mud huts in the rainforests and believed in spirits and in magic now live in neat houses in a modern city, and their children eagerly go to schools and colleges whenever they have the opportunity.

Many young Africans, instead of becoming hunters and farmers in the old tradition, are moving to the cities to work in factories, mines, and offices. Some of them become doctors, nurses, and teachers. Some become journalists, lawyers, and political leaders.

Africa today is a land of great contrast and conflict between primitive and modern ways of life. But its future is promising.

Nurses' Training School at Sekondi, Ghana, is an example of modern Africa's concern for health.

British Information Service

The building may be made of clay and the roof of tin, but it houses doctors fighting malaria.

One of the most important things that is happening is the gradual conquest of the diseases that ravage the continent. Millions of square miles of land have been cleared of the tsetse fly, meaning that men and animals can safely live and work there. Malaria, the most widespread of all African diseases, is being checked. In Léopoldville, Belgian Congo, for instance, airplanes spray the city regularly with DDT to kill the mosquitoes which carry malaria. Intensive research is going on in an effort to find a way to conquer bilharziasis.

Many countries are building new hospitals, training doctors and nurses, and teaching Africans the essentials of cleanliness and good health. Missionaries from Europe and America devote their lives to providing better medical care for Africans.

Another important development is the growth of transportation. More and better roads and railways are being built through the swamps and rainforests, and even across the Sahara Desert. Airplanes are bringing within reach even the most inaccessible places in Africa, and increasing numbers of landing strips are being built to serve remote districts.

Schools and colleges are being built to educate young Africans so that they can help to lead their people into the future. But education is still possible only for a lucky minority. It is estimated that nearly 90 per cent of all Africans south of the Sahara cannot read or write.

It may hurt a bit, but these youngsters are proud of the anti-tuberculosis vaccinations.

Young Africans in Kenya study modern science in the Royal Technical College, Nairobi.

A Nigerian sounds an oversized horn to announce the arrival of a plane at Kano's airport.

Science, too, is contributing to Africa's future. Engineers are building huge dams in strategic spots along the continent's mighty rivers. These dams will help to control dangerous floods, to store water for irrigation of the land, and to provide electric power for the new industries that are springing up.

And, finally, a continent that seemed to be poverty-stricken is revealing itself as a land rich in many things the rest of the world needs. Valuable minerals—copper, uranium, cobalt, tin, manganese, and all the others we have read about—have been discovered. Huge plants are being built to process them. Railways and roads will have to be improved to transport them. Seaports will have to be enlarged to ship them to other nations. Millions of Africans will earn their living doing all these things.

In addition, new methods of farming and of conserving the soil will make it possible to grow many new crops, and to increase the yields of presently grown crops many times over.

In terms of land and people and natural resources, Africa is potentially the richest continent of all.

But Africa has problems in its future, too. No people can undergo such far-reaching changes in so short a time without becoming confused and troubled.

Airplanes provide speedy connections between Nairobi, East Africa's air center, and major world cities.

Africans want to control their own destiny, to chart their own future, to be free of control by other nations. This spirit is called nationalism. Many African countries have won their independence in recent years: Tunisia, Morocco, Egypt, Sudan, Ghana, Guinea, and Nigeria. But there are still huge areas where Africans are ruled by outsiders. In some of these regions Africans are being given more opportunity to govern themselves. But some African leaders feel things are moving too slowly, and are pressing for faster action.

In a few regions of Africa the white man segregates the black man. In the Union of South Africa, as we have seen, complete separation between the races is official policy. In other countries, Africans may work with white men, but may not live in the same neighborhood, or eat in the same restaurant. In still other countries, there is no "color bar" at all.

Unless understanding between the races can be achieved, bitter feelings and even the danger of open revolt can be a serious obstacle to Africa's progress.

Another major problem in Africa's future is that modern democratic ideas are in conflict with the slowly dying patterns of tribal life. The tribe was a man's family. He had certain responsibilities to it. There were certain traditions to be observed.

Joe Barnell—Shostal

An Egyptian tractor crew works beside a native-built irrigation canal in Egypt's Liberation Province, a major land-reform and reclamation project.

Below left: Egyptian steelworkers watch the tapping of the furnace in Egypt's first steel plant.

Below right: a native dredge crew widens the Suez canal, now entirely Egyptian-managed.

Bob Crone—Annan Photo Features

Bob Crone—Annan Photo Features

A government-sponsored traveling puppet show teaches personal hygiene to children in Ghana. Such programs help improve living standards.

Stephanie Dinkins—FLO

He had a definite place where he belonged. There was security in belonging to the tribe, as there is in belonging to a family.

But democracy emphasizes the individual, and the young African, caught midway in his journey between tribalism and democracy, is often confused and puzzled.

There are other problems in Africa's future. Many millions of people are still terribly poor. The population is growing so fast there may not be food enough to feed everyone. The leaders of African countries rushing to independence may not yet be capable of intelligent self-government. And finally, the continent is so rich a prize that Communism may try to influence Africans to turn their backs on the countries and the men of the free world.

Today's young people will watch the unfolding of this drama as Africa moves ahead into its exciting future—a future that will be important to the whole world.

In the Cameroons, a volunteer teacher helps the women of one village learn to read and spell.

Leon V. Kofod—Monkmeyer

A fetish priest, representative of Africa's old order, squats in front of a "Freedom" slogan.

Tribal fetishes and talking drums signal the start of a political rally in independent Ghana.

Symbolizing the hope of all Africans for a free future is the Arch of Independence in Accra, Ghana.

AFRICA—FACTS AND FIGURES

PRINCIPAL COUNTRIES AND COLONIES: AREA AND POPULATION

Country	Area in sq. miles	Population (est. 1960)
Algeria	846,120	10,753,600
Angola	481,350	4,511,600
Belgian Congo	904,750	14,909,400
Cameroon	200,570	5,037,800
Ethiopia	395,000	18,000,000
French Community States	3,004,635	32,782,800
Ghana	91,690	5,073,000
Guinea	95,350	2,950,500
Kenya	224,960	6,611,400
Liberia	43,000	1,500,000
Libya	679,400	1,189,600
Morocco	159,000	10,691,600
Mozambique	297,730	6,435,300
Nigeria	338,600	36,606,800
Rhodesia and Nyasaland, Federation of	480,000	8,384,500
Sierra Leone	27,970	2,238,600
Somalia	198,000	1,341,400
South-West Africa	317,725	612,600
Sudan	971,500	11,000,000
Tanganyika	362,690	9,368,000
Togo	21,500	1,137,800
Tunisia	48,300	4,070,700
Uganda	93,980	5,630,700
U. of South Africa	472,490	15,211,000
United Arab Republic (Egypt)	386,200	27,675,000

LARGE CITIES AND THEIR POPULATION

City and Country	Est. Pop.
Cairo, Egypt	2,600,000
Alexandria, Egypt	1,200,000
Johannesburg, U. of South Africa	1,006,000
Casablanca, Morocco	682,000
Tunis, Tunisia	680,000
Cape Town, U. of South Africa	687,000
Durban, U. of South Africa	591,300
Ibadan, Nigeria	500,000
Addis Ababa, Ethiopia	500,000
Léopoldville, Belgian Congo	370,490
Algiers, Algeria	361,285

City and Country	Population
Pretoria, U. of South Africa	327,200
Lagos, Nigeria	320,000
Oran, Algeria	299,018
Asyut, Egypt	250,000
Marrakech, Morocco	220,000
Brazzaville, Republic of the Congo	205,000
Salisbury, Southern Rhodesia	200,000
Nairobi, Kenya	186,000
Dakar, Republic of Senegal	185,000

HIGHEST MOUNTAINS AND THEIR ELEVATIONS

Mountain and Country	Height in feet
Kilimanjaro, Tanganyika	19,565
Kenya, Kenya	17,040
Ruwenzori, Belgian Congo	16,795
Ras Dashan, Ethiopia	15,160
Elgon, Kenya	14,178
Toubkal, Morocco	13,665
Birhan, Ethiopia	13,625
Tala, Ethiopia	13,451
Cameroon, Cameroon	13,350
Emi Koussi, Republic of Chad	11,204

LARGEST LAKES AND THEIR AREAS

Lake and Region of Africa	Area in sq. miles
Victoria, Central Africa	26,828
Tanganyika, Central Africa	12,700
Nyasa, Central Africa	11,000
Chad, Central Africa	8,000
Rudolf, Central Africa	3,500
Albert, Central Africa	2,064
Tana, Central Africa	1,400
Leopold II, Central Africa	900

LONGEST RIVERS AND THEIR LENGTH

River and Region of Africa	Length in miles
Nile, Northern and Central Africa	4,150
Congo, Central Africa	2,900
Niger, Central Africa	2,600
Zambezi, Southern Africa	1,600
Ubangi-Uélé, Central Africa	1,400
Orange, Southern Africa	1,300
Kasai, Central Africa	1,100
Limpopo, Southern Africa	1,000
Okovanggo, Southern Africa	1,000